CountryLiving

DECK THE HALLS

*Christmas Notecards, Labels, Ornaments,
and Other Festive & Fun Projects*

EDITED BY

Katy McColl

ILLUSTRATIONS BY

Rebecca Schmidt of Mr. Boddington's Studio

HEARST BOOKS
New York

HEARST BOOKS
New York

An Imprint of Sterling Publishing
387 Park Avenue South
New York, NY 10016

Design by Lana Le of Wooly Pear Design

10 9 8 7 6 5 4 3 2 1

Published by Hearst Books
A division of Sterling Publishing Co., Inc.
387 Park Avenue South, New York, NY 10016

Country Living is a registered trademark of Hearst Communications, Inc.

www.countryliving.com

For information about custom editions, special sales, premium and corporate purchases, please contact Sterling Special Sales Department at 800-805-5489 or specialsales@sterlingpublishing.com.

Distributed in Canada by Sterling Publishing
c/o Canadian Manda Group, 165 Dufferin Street
Toronto, Ontario, Canada M6K 3H6

Distributed in Australia by Capricorn Link (Australia) Pty. Ltd.
P.O. Box 704, Windsor, NSW 2756 Australia

Manufactured in China

Sterling ISBN 978-1-58816-923-5

PHOTOGRAPHY CREDITS

Lucas Allen: 98, 126, 162
Christopher Baker: 54, 58, 59 (both photos), 60 (both photos), 61
Amber S. Clark: 23, 26
Colin Cooke: 27 (both photos)
Joseph De Leo: 99
Tara Donne: 100-101, 102, 103
Don Freeman: 8 left, 90
John Granen: 134 bottom right, 136 top, 138 bottom left, 140
Aimée Herring: 92 (both photos)
Lisa Hubbard: 104, 134 top right
Max Kim-Bee: 2
Library of Congress: 141 top right and bottom left, 142 top left and bottom right, 143 (all birds except bottom left), 144 (all birds except bottom right)
Kate Mathis: 7 left, 14, 17, 18, 19, 20, 21, 24, 25, 28, 30 top
Debra McClinton: 166, 167 (both photos)
Keith Scott Morton: 133
Laura Moss: 97
Kana Okada: 15
Steven Randazzo: 94, 132
Victor Schrager: 95, 128, 129 (all photos), 131 left, 134 left, 136 bottom, 137
Tony Stamolis: 6
Kirsten Strecker: 64, 65, 66, 67, 68
STUDIO D: Lara Robby: 7 right, 16, 29, 32, 56, 62, 63, 130, 139, 175, 176; **Addie Juell:** 96, 135 left; **Philip Friedman:** 8 right, 12, 13, 31 bottom right, 168, 169, 170, 172, 173, 174; **Karl Juengel:** 22; **J. Muckle:** 30 (bottom three photos), 31 (all photos except bottom right); **Jesus Ayala:** 164-165 (all photos)
Björn Wallander: 131 right, 135 right, 138 top right
Anna Williams: 10
Courtesy of Adrienne Wong: 171 (illustration)

Back Cover
(clockwise from top right): **Lara Robby/ Studio D, Lara Robby/Studio D, Debra McClinton, Kate Mathis**

CONTENTS

WELCOME

How excited am I about this book? Just picture a kid on Christmas Eve. Only now—instead of eagerly anticipating my very own stereo and rollerskates—I can't wait for you to open our latest, and greatest, holiday guide.

Inside, you'll discover scores of DIY gift ideas, from gilded pinecone necklaces to irresistible honey-flavored granola. All yield presents as polished as any stuff you'd find in a store. The main difference: You'll spend a lot less for sweet somethings that mean much, much more—because you made 'em yourself.

We've also packed the following pages with clever decorating and wrapping how-tos (who knew crayon shavings and tissue paper could look so sophisticated?), as well as sage entertaining advice. Read on to find out why you should splurge on scotch, skimp on vodka, and always keep pistachios on hand.

As if that weren't enough, *Country Living* conspired with the artists at Mr. Boddington's Studio to create some 90 pages of pull-outs, including beautifully illustrated gift tags, ornaments, recipe cards, stickers, and the cutest craft templates ever. (Seriously, I dare you to toss that little sheep silhouette after completing the farmhouse mug project on page 17.)

All we ask in return is that you have not just a happy holiday, but a truly inspired, joyous one—the kind money simply cannot buy.

SARAH GRAY MILLER
Editor-in-Chief, *Country Living*

LET THE MERRY-MAKING BEGIN!

SINCE THE ADVENT OF ADVENT CALENDARS—AND PERHAPS LONG BEFORE— the anticipation that builds as the house fills with holiday sounds, sights, and smells has become a huge part of the joy of Christmas. Decking the halls and other traditions take on added pleasure, because unlike other holidays that come and go in a single fleeting day, Christmas encompasses an entire sparkling season. And what a whirlwind it can be—full of parties, presents, candlelit dinners, fragrant greenery, lustrous ribbons, and jingling bells.

Rather than weighing down your to-do list with formal advice and complex kitchen challenges, we're here to help you celebrate with a practical how-to holiday guide dedicated solely to the fun stuff. With an emphasis on simple recipes and stylish DIY projects—some super-quick and none excessively tricky—this book is designed to help you get the most out of the most wonderful time of year, without draining all your free time or your bank account.

✳ **Dozens of presents to make and give**— from playful woodland tote bags to nautical-chic paperweights, even a Victorian-style terrarium for hothouse

flowers. (Go ahead and covet some of these treasures for yourself—and bah humbug to anyone who says otherwise.)

* **Recipes for crowd-pleasing treats,** like golden honey granola and melt-in-your-mouth caramels, will enable you to remember everyone on your list in the sweetest way possible. Plus: Construct an edible cottage out of gingerbread and jelly beans.

* **Adorable place cards and napkin rings,** along with ideas for creative centerpieces and mantle makeovers, will bring jolly cheer to the dining room—not to mention the no-stress cocktail shindig we've mapped out on page 100.

* **Decorating the rest of the house** will be a dream, thanks to inventive wreaths, kicky plaid tree skirts, and winning strategies for displaying a flurry of greeting cards. With ideas for glamorous ornaments that cost just pennies a pop—plus dozens of ready-to-hang options starting on page 141—you won't want to stop at a single tree. (And why would you when every table can hold an evergreen of its own?)

* **Finally, we show you how to turn crayon** shavings and newsprint—among other novel trappings—into elegant wrapping styles.

All this creativity will surely boost your spirits and bring out the sugar-cookie-loving, mistletoe-hanging, stay-up-all-night-in-anticipation kid within. And that's precisely the point. A stunningly stylish holiday minus the stress of complicated preparations? Ho, ho, ho, we'll drink to that!

CHAPTER

ONE

THE JOY OF GIVING

●>>> <<<●

Adorable Handmade Holiday Gifts

THE 22 PRESENTS ON THE FOLLOWING PAGES PROVE THAT YOU DON'T
have to spend big to give well. These simple projects turn inexpensive and overlooked
materials into scene-stealing stars—drawing upon the potential of vintage handkerchiefs, recycled knit sweaters, fallen pine cones, and hardware store dropcloths
to create thoughtful and enchanting presents. As a bonus, you'll be able to skip all
those harried trips to the mall and instead spend your afternoons at home crafting—
preferably with your favorite carols cranked up and a glass of eggnog close at hand.
Plus, watching your friends and families unwrap their bounty on the big day will
take on a special sparkle when the treasures in question are ones you made yourself.
Ready to get inspired? Turn the page.

Shake Things Up with Custom Snow-globes

For a cooler-than-cool stocking stuffer, create a mini winter wonderland with a snow-globe kit. Here's how to get the ball rolling:

SUPPLIES

Snow-globe kit (or Mason jar)

Toy(s) to put inside

Sheets of model-train "grass"

Waterproof epoxy

Clear lacquer

Distilled water

Decorative ribbon

Glue dots

❶ Decide what you'd like to put in your globe (we chose a pair of fancy cupcake toppers), keeping in mind that plastic and ceramic work best underwater.

❷ If desired, cover your globe's base. Since ours feature outdoor scenes, we used sheets of model-train "grass" adhered with waterproof epoxy. Spray the base with clear lacquer; let dry.

❸ Position your figure on the base; affix with epoxy.

❹ Once the epoxy has dried, attach the dome to the base and fill with distilled water and the included snow, following the kit's instructions. To hide the seam where the base and dome meet, use glue dots to affix a decorative ribbon around the globe's circumference. Looks like it's a small world, after all.

Find adorable labels for all your presents on pages 45–51.

Bathing Beauties

Enjoy some good clean fun with these easy-to-make soaps, shaped using animal-themed cookie cutters.

SUPPLIES

Medium-size chunk of melt-and-pour glycerin

Animal-shaped cookie cutter(s)

Food coloring

Rubbing alcohol

Knife

1 For your own menagerie, heat a medium-size chunk of melt-and-pour glycerin in the microwave. While it melts, place the cutters in deep metal baking pans.

2 Once the glycerin liquefies, tint it with food coloring, then pour it in the middle of each cutter so the glycerin fills it to the top (use only one soap color per pan, in case any spills over).

3 Spray the glycerin with rubbing alcohol and let sit until it hardens.

4 Using a knife, cut around the inside of the cookie cutter, then gently press the soap through to release it. Wild!

Unexpected Uses for Vintage Handkerchiefs

These crafts breathe new life into old-fashioned linens.

SUPPLIES

Vintage handkerchiefs

Needle

Thread

Buttons

Dried lavender

To MAKE A TABLE RUNNER, measure the length of your table (plus overhang) to determine how many hankies you'll need (we used ten 12-inch squares for an 82-inch-long table). To connect the first two, flip them pattern side down, overlapping the edges by about ⅜ inch; pin, then stitch together. Continue attaching handkerchiefs in this manner until the runner is complete. <

To MAKE A SACHET, cut a four-inch square from a hankie. With the pattern side up, fold three corners toward the square's center. Hand-stitch the sides together. Turn the sachet inside out, press, and sew a decorative button atop the flap. Fill the pouch with dried lavender, then secure the flap with some hidden hand-sewn stitches. ʌ

Turn a Motto into a Work of Art

Reward a great quote (we cribbed from The Wizard of Oz) with the deluxe gallery treatment.

1 Lay a piece of poster board on a flat surface. Use letter stencils to spell out the phrase of your choice on the board, experimenting until you find a placement you like. (Use a ruler and pencil to mark horizontal lines for guidance.)

2 Spell out the phrase backward, then flip the stencils over (you'll be turning the board over when you're done, and the words will then read correctly). Trace the letters onto the board with a pencil.

3 Carefully cut out the letters with an X-Acto knife, then use hem tape (such as Heat 'n Bond) to affix a patterned piece of fabric to the poster board. Flip the poster board over to reveal the finished artwork, then frame.

SUPPLIES

Poster board

Letter stencils

X-Acto knife

Hem tape

Patterned fabric

Frame to fit board

Redefine "Farm to Table"

Look no further than the nearest pasture for inspiration to dress up plain dishware.

SUPPLIES

Mugs

Template

Contact paper

Paint brush

PermEnamel paint

Cotton swab

To duplicate these mugs, punch out the perforated shapes by artist Jennifer Rizzo on pages 33–36. For each shape, place atop a small piece of contact paper and outline it in pencil. Cut out with a craft knife, and discard or repurpose the contact paper critter as a sticker. (You can save the cardboard template for future use or punch a hole through it and use as a gift tag.) Peel away the contact paper backing and affix the stencil to a clean, dry mug, making sure to center the image. Following the package directions, use a soft brush to fill in the outline with dishwasher-safe PermEnamel paint; let set for a few minutes. Carefully remove the contact paper, clean up any edges with a damp cotton swab, and allow the paint to cure for 10 days.

Use the stencils on pages 33–36 to create these barnyard beauties.

Transform Nature's Bounty into Glittering Charms

Throughout fall and early winter, pinecones and acorns are free for the taking. And in less than an hour, you can cast your findings in 18-karat gold—spray paint, that is.

SUPPLIES

Acorns or hemlock pinecones

Hot Glue gun

Jump ring(s)

Gold paint

Clear sealer

Golden chains

1 Gather or purchase acorns and hemlock pinecones.

2 Use hot glue to affix a jump ring to the top of each acorn or pine-cone, near the back.

3 After the glue dries, carefully spray the objects with one coat of gold paint.

4 Let paint dry for 20 minutes, then spray the charm with clear sealer; allow 10 minutes to dry.

5 String the charms onto golden chains.

Lend Plain Totes Animal Appeal

Here's how to turn a plain canvas tote into a cute woodland-themed carryall:

SUPPLIES

Animal templates,
pages 37-42

Fabrics

Iron-on adhesive

Plain canvas
tote bag

Buttons

Needle

Thread

*Find stencils
for these cute
critters on
pages 37–42.*

❶ Punch out the animal templates—including acorns and antlers—from pages 37–42. Using our photo as a guide, pick a mix of fabrics and place the template on the fabrics; trace and cut out.

❷ Next, trace the template onto iron-on adhesive and cut inside the lines so the adhesive shapes are slightly smaller than the fabric ones. Following the package instructions, iron adhesive to the back of the fabric.

❸ Remove the adhesive's backing. Working pattern side up, center the animal's fabric body on a plain canvas tote bag and iron in place. Follow with the other pieces of the animal, again using our photo for guidance. Finish by sewing on button eyes for the owl and squirrel.

Ribbon Bookmarks with Real Charm

Jewelry designer Andrea Singarella (andreasingarella.com) fashioned these bibliophilic baubles for just a few dollars each.

To assemble your own, cut **velvet ribbon** into 9-inch lengths. Purchase **ribbon clamps** the same width as your ribbon, then use **flat-nose jewelry pliers** to affix clamps to both ends of each ribbon. Finish by attaching charms, trinkets, or **vintage earrings** to the clamps with **jump rings**.

Branch Out with Leaf Coasters

These elegant and rustic drink perches will impress all your friends.

Saw a **tree limb branch** (3 inches in diameter) into slices about ¾ inch thick—or have a hardware store do it for you—and lightly sand the top and bottom of each wood disk. Create the leaf motifs shown by pressing inked **leaf-shaped stamps** onto wood. Let dry for five minutes, then coat the stamped sides with a protective **matte sealer**. Allow 15 minutes of drying time before using.

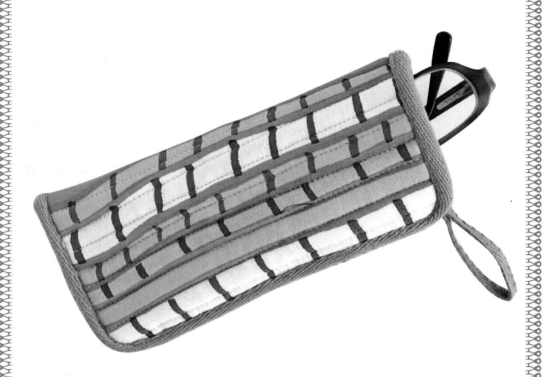

Save Those Specs!

Even if you've never tried out a sewing machine, you can whip up this snappy eyeglass case from Jodi Kahn, author of Simply Sublime Bags: 30 No-Sew, Low-Sew Projects.

SUPPLIES

Quilted pot holder

Needle

Thread

Just fold a quilted pot holder in half, hand-stitch the edges together, and present the resulting padded pouch to your favorite four-eyes.

Period Pinups

Give utilitarian bulletin boards personality by disguising them as artful silhouettes.

SUPPLIES

Templates (pages 43-44), enlarged by 300%

11"x17" corkboard

Self-healing mat

X-Acto knife

Flat black spray paint

Adhesive mounting strips

❶ Punch out our templates from pages 43–44, then use a photocopier to enlarge each of them by 300 percent.

❷ Center each enlarged profile on an 11-by-17-inch corkboard, available at craft stores by the roll, and trace around it with a pen.

❸ Working on a protected surface, such as a chopping block or self-healing mat, slowly score the pen lines with an X-Acto knife. Because of the cork's thickness, you'll need to go over each cut several times before slicing all the way through.

❹ Spray the silhouettes with two coats of flat black paint, let dry overnight, and hang with adhesive mounting strips. Very *Pride & Prejudice.*

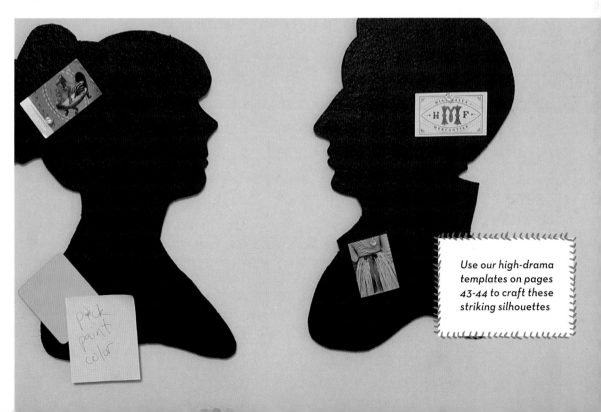

Use our high-drama templates on pages 43-44 to craft these striking silhouettes

Copy-and-Paste Desk Organizers

These cleverly decoupaged containers, covered in photorealistic images of the very supplies they hold, will cause the recipient's office mates to do a double take.

FOR THE PUSHPIN BOX, scatter pins on a color copier and lay blue paper on top of them. Copy; then cut the image to fit the lid and base of a small box (both the box and the cylinder at left came from containerstore.com). Spread rubber cement on the image's underside and the container. Once the glue gets tacky, affix the paper, smoothing out any air bubbles, and let dry.

TO MAKE THE PENCIL CUP, color-copy a row of pencils onto heavy paper. Cut the image to fit a 6-inch-high cylinder, trimming off the erasers, as shown. Adhere the paper following the directions above.

FOR THE SCISSORS REST, color-copy your shears onto a sheet of paper, then cut out the image. Cover a small dish with a coat of matte glue, and let dry. Paint a second coat; then, while it's wet, affix the image. Let dry. Complete this, and projects above, by coating them with a thin layer of glue; repeat two to three times, letting dry between coats, until well sealed.

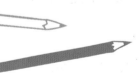

SUPPLIES

Push pins

Blue paper

Small box

Rubber cement

6-inch-high cardboard cylinder

Pencils

Small dish

Matte glue

ahoy matey

A Desk Accessory
Worth its Weight in Gold

For this nifty nautical paperweight, artist Brittni Mehlhoff of papernstitchblog.com relied on a pair of silicone candle molds. Consider giving this shipshape token to anyone who could use some heavy-duty organizing help.

SUPPLIES

Rubber gloves

Pottery plaster powder

Silicone candle molds

Clear shellac

Gold liquid leaf paint

Superglue

❶ Following package instructions (and wearing rubber gloves), mix pottery plaster powder and cold water. Stir continuously until the mixture reaches the consistency of pancake batter.

❷ Slowly pour into each mold (we found the anchor mold at firstimpressionsmolds.com and the round base mold at thesage.com) until the mixture reaches just to the mold's top. Let dry for one hour.

❸ Gently remove the hardened weights from their molds. Let the plaster set for one day, then spray the front and back of each weight with a clear shellac. Allow an hour of drying time, then paint the weights with gold liquid leaf; let dry for another hour. Coat each piece again with shellac and, after an hour, attach the anchor to the base using Superglue.

Brooch the Subject

Repurpose old pins and brooches to create quick and cheery baubles for the refrigerator.

Vintage pins are such a tempting site at flea markets, especially since they usually cost only a couple of dollars a pop. But how often do you actually wear a brooch? Instead of letting these baubles gather dust in your jewelry box, turn them into refrigerator magnets: Use a pair of **needle-nose pliers** to remove the pin hardware from the back of each brooch (most fittings will come off easily); then affix a **superstrong magnet** with a small bead of glue—like **Superglue**. Let dry overnight. Grocery lists have never looked more glam!

Knit Wit

Transform old sweaters into cozy gifts with these two wallet-friendly projects.

To create a hothouse vase for blossoms slip a **detached sweater sleeve** over a **jar or bottle**, lining up the cuff with either the top or bottom edge, and **hot-glue** in place. Cut the wool long enough to cover the entire vessel, then secure with more glue. >

Basic bangle bracelets get dressed for the season in soft yarn (and, if you use jewelry you already own, they cost next to nothing). Just cover a **plastic cuff** in a strip of **chunky knit,** then hot-glue in place on the inside. ∨

Treat Basic Slippers to a Sweet Makeover

Use a dish towel to bring serious style to standard housewear with this idea from Jodi Kahn.

SUPPLIES

Patterned dish towel

Fabric glue

Waffle-weave slippers

Needle

Thread

➊ From a patterned dish towel, cut a strip that measures 8 inches across the bottom, 6¼ inches along the top, and 4¼ inches on the sides, with the motif you wish to highlight centered in the middle. Fold the top and bottom edges under ½ inch and the sides under 1 inch, and iron to create creases.

➋ Spread a thin layer of fabric glue evenly over the strip's back side and press it down over the band of a waffle-weave slipper. Let dry for 20 minutes. Repeat with other slipper. To add a decorative border, hand-stitch along the top and bottom edges.

The Perfect Place to Jot Down Your Grocery List

Recycle pretty paper bags into journals in this project by artist Regina Lord of creativekismet.com.

SUPPLIES

Paper grocery bags

X-Acto knife

Paper clips

Awl

Needle

Embroidery thread

1 For each bag, remove the handles (we used one from Trader Joe's) if necessary, then carefully open the bottom and side seams. Iron on high to flatten the paper.

2 Using a ruler and X-Acto knife, measure and cut the bag into six 12-by-8-inch pieces for a large book, or eight 8-by-5-inch sheets for a small version.

3 Stack the papers, plain side facing up, and fold in half.

4 With the book closed, use a pencil to mark half-inch increments along the fold.

5 Hold the stack together with paper clips, then use an awl to poke a hole through the spine at each pencil mark.

6 Starting at the bottom, sew a running or a coptic stitch with embroidery thread up the journal's spine through the holes you just made. If you use a running stitch, leave a 3-inch tail of thread at the top of the spine; then, using another piece of thread, stitch down through the spine. Tie the tails at the top in a double knot.

Build a Picture-Perfect Terrarium

Give your ferns, orchids, and other hothouse plants a lovely place to call home with this photoframe oasis developed by C.J. Hughes of theupcycler.com.

SUPPLIES

Eight frames (four 5"x 7," two 8"x 10," and two 11"x 14")

Drill

Screws*

2" mending plates

Corner brackets

Two 1" utility hinges

Gloves

Wood filler

White paint

Paint brush

*The screws you use should correspond with your drill bit. We suggest a 3/32" bit and #6 x 1/2" wood screws.

Remove the backs and glass from all eight frames. Lightly sand each frame's surface.

Align an 11" x 14" frame with an 8" x 10" one as shown. Drill one hole near the top and one near the bottom, through the larger frame and halfway into the smaller; screw together.* Repeat with other 11" x 14" and 8" x 10" frames.

Arrange the two L's you've created, as shown. Attach them to each other using the same method described in Step 2 to form the terrarium's base.

Place two 5" x 7" frames facedown. Align a 2" mending plate at each end of the frames, as shown. Drill pilot holes and secure with screws.* Repeat with the two remaining frames.

Align the two sets of 5" x 7" frames as shown. Attach a corner bracket inside each end of the eave, using the method described in Step 4.

Line the resulting roof up with the base, as shown. Place two 1" utility hinges, spaced evenly apart, over the joint where the pieces meet. Drill holes and screw together.*

Trace the inside of an eave on paper. Cut out, and trace the resulting triangle onto a piece of ½"-thick plywood. Repeat; then cut the wood.

Fit the cut wood into each end of the roof. Attach by predrilling holes from the outside of the roof into the triangles and securing with screws.*

Wearing gloves for safety, smooth wood filler over the terrarium's exterior, filling in the joints and covering the screw holes. Let dry for several hours; then lightly sand.

Paint the piece white. For a distressed finish, apply a dark furniture polish over the paint after it dries. Let sit for a few minutes; then buff off.

Replace the glass from the bottom up. Place hot glue in the corners of each frame, pop the pane in, and run glue around each frame's inside edge.

Lift the terrarium's lid to fit your favorite plants inside. Set by a sunny window and admire how your mini garden grows.

Show Your Stripes

Painted lines transform humble canvas into a tablecloth with French country flavor.

SUPPLIES

Drop cloth

1/4-inch grout tape

Fabric paint

Paper plate

Paint brush

Paper towel

1 Wash and tumble dry a natural-colored canvas drop cloth from the hardware store—ours measured 6 by 9 feet—a few times to soften the fabric.

2 Lay the cloth flat. Run a strip of 1/4-inch grout tape down the middle of the fabric widthwise. Then run two additional pieces of tape on each side of the first, spacing them 1/4 inch apart (you'll have five strips total).

3 Squirt some red fabric paint onto a paper plate and dab a brush in it, off-loading any extra paint onto a paper towel. Working in short strokes, lightly brush the paint on the cloth between the taped areas to catch the grain of the canvas.

4 Continue to layer the pigment until it appears as dark as desired. Remove the tape once the paint has dried according to the package instructions.

LET'S GET TO WORK!

FARM-TO-TABLE MUGS *Use these punch-out animals to make the mugs as instructed on page 17. The critters can also double as gift tags—just create an opening with a hole punch to thread a ribbon through.*

FARM-TO-TABLE MUGS

FARM-TO-TABLE MUGS

FARM-TO-TABLE MUGS

WOODLAND-THEMED TOTES *Punch out this stencil to make the totes as instructed on page 19. The critters can also double as a gift tag—just use glue to attach the parts and a hole punch to create an opening to thread a ribbon through.*

WOODLAND-THEMED TOTES

WOODLAND-THEMED TOTES

WOODLAND-THEMED TOTES

WOODLAND-THEMED TOTES

WOODLAND-THEMED TOTES

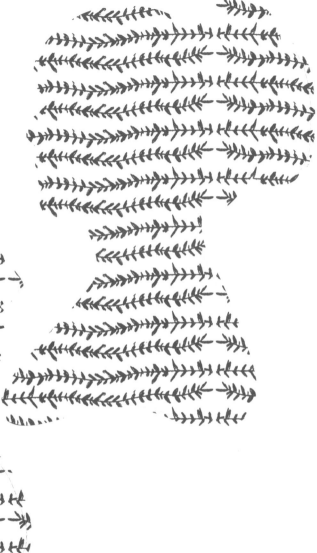

PERIOD PINUPS *Punch out and enlarge these silhouettes on a copier to make the bulletin boards as instructed on page 23. When you're finished, this silhouette can also be used to dress up a package: just glue atop a wrapped box.*

PERIOD PINUPS

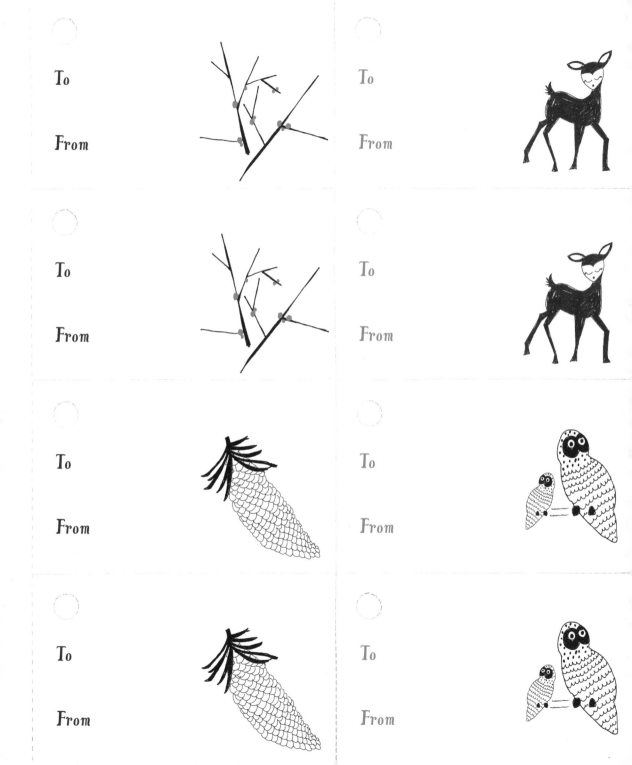

To

From

To

From

To

From

To

From

To

From

To

From

To

From

To

From

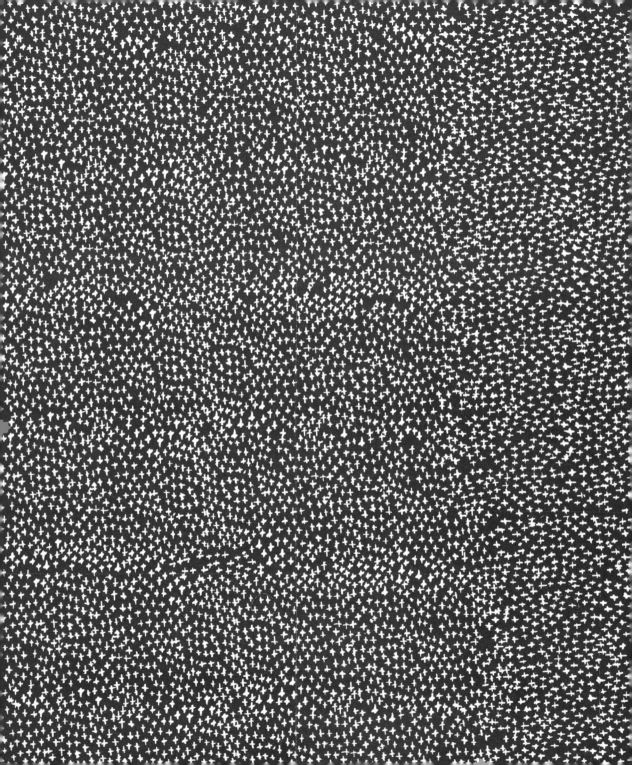

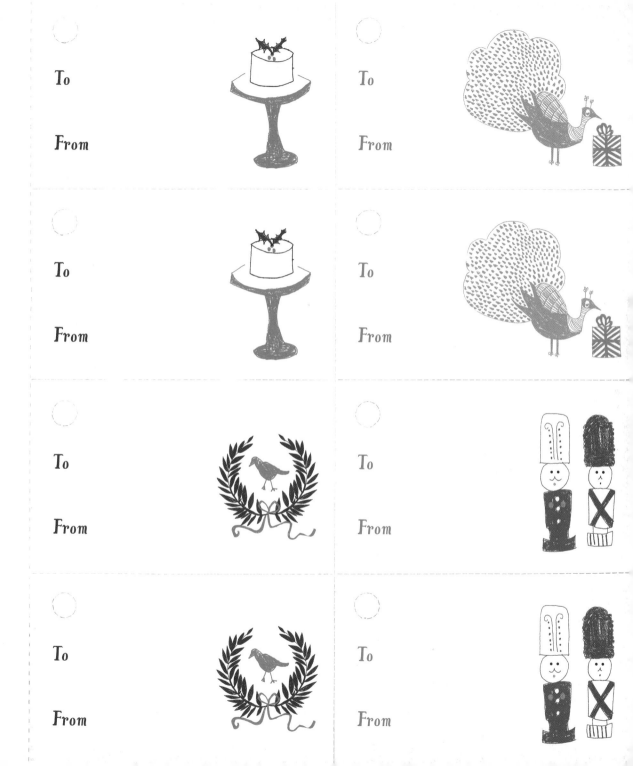

To

From

To

From

To

From

To

From

To

From

To

From

To

From

To

From

To:

From:

To:

From:

To:

From:

To:

From:

To:

From:

To:

From:

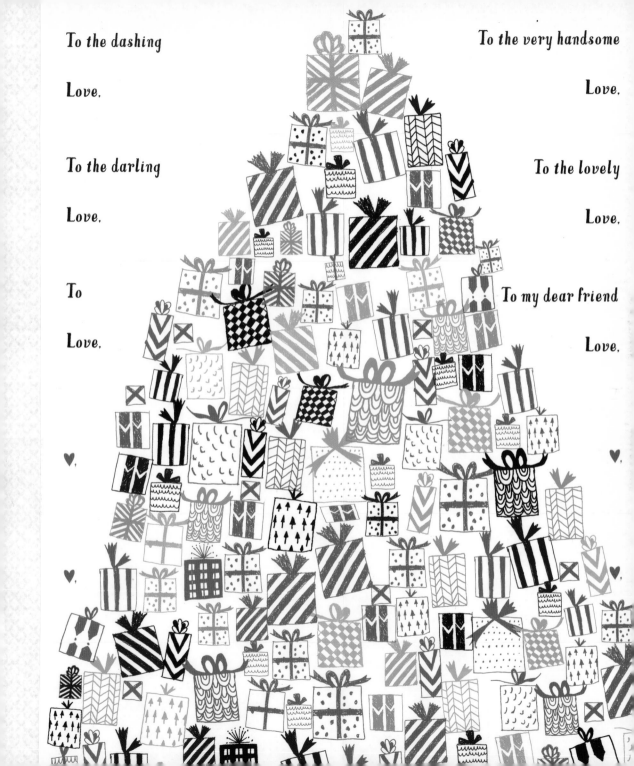

To the dashing

Love,

To the darling

Love,

To

Love,

♥,

♥,

To the very handsome

Love,

To the lovely

Love,

To my dear friend

Love,

♥,

CHAPTER

TWO

DELICIOUS GIFTS
from the
CHRISTMAS KITCHEN

●》》》 《《《●

Tasty Treats to Make and Share

BELIEF IN SANTA MAY CHANGE OVER THE YEARS, BUT THE THRILL OF gooey chocolate and caramel endures forever. That's why we've gathered our best goodies into one exceptionally delicious go-to file—including recipes for playful pastry puzzles like the gingerbread boy on page 57, and a hardworking brownie batter that yields five different treats. These delicacies will sweeten the days of all the folks who bring joy to your life—from friends and neighbors to the miracle worker who cuts your hair. Memories are made in the kitchen, and nothing fills a house with warmth more than fresh-baked cookies or the clatter of mixers and rolling pins, so turn on the oven and let's get cooking.

Find labels for your home-baked presents on pages 85-87. SWEET!

Gingerbread Cookie Dough

A twist on the traditional gingerbread boy, this puzzle's good enough to eat.

MAKES EIGHT 4-BY-6-INCH PUZZLES **WORKING TIME** 45 MIN. **TOTAL TIME** 5½ HR.

2½ cups all-purpose flour

1 tablespoon ground ginger

½ teaspoon ground cloves

¼ teaspoon salt

1 stick unsalted butter

½ cup dark corn syrup

¼ cup dark brown sugar

¼ cup granulated sugar

1 In a large bowl, combine flour, ground ginger, ground cloves, and salt and set aside.

2 In a medium saucepan over medium heat, place butter, corn syrup, brown sugar, and granulated sugar and stir until butter melts and sugars dissolve.

3 Add butter mixture to flour mixture and stir with a wooden spoon until combined.

4 Divide dough in half and cover in plastic wrap; pat into ½-inch-thick squares. Chill until very firm, 4 hours or overnight, then follow directions below.

THE KEY TO THIS PUZZLING PASTRY?

First, roll out dough on a well-floured surface to ⅛ inch thick. Cut out eight 4-by-6-inch rectangles. Working with one rectangle at a time (keep others in fridge), use a 2½-inch-tall cookie cutter to punch out a gingerbread boy from center. With a paring knife, cut 8 to 12 pieces from around gingerbread boy to create a puzzle, as shown at left. Using a spatula, transfer pieces to a parchment-lined baking sheet and refrigerate for 20 minutes. Repeat with remaining rectangles. Preheat oven to 350° F.

Remove puzzles from refrigerator and use a knife to gently separate cutout pieces from one another (about ½ inch) so that they don't fuse in the oven. Brush gingerbread boy lightly with beaten egg white and sprinkle with sugar. Bake 12 minutes. Let cool completely.

Brownies: One Batter, Five Ways

An unbeatable mix of decadent goodness, these hardworking treats earn their rich flavor from bittersweet chocolate, brown sugar, vanilla extract, and unsweetened cocoa powder. Here are five simple ways to tart up this original recipe.

BASIC BROWNIE BATTER

WORKING TIME 10 MIN. **TOTAL TIME** 10 MIN.

1 stick unsalted butter, plus more for pans

8 ounces bittersweet chocolate, chopped

¾ cup granulated sugar

½ cup packed light-brown sugar

3 large eggs

1½ teaspoons vanilla extract

¾ teaspoon salt

½ cup all-purpose flour, plus more for pans

3 tablespoons unsweetened cocoa

In a heatproof bowl over a pot of simmering water, melt butter. Add chocolate and stir until melted. Remove bowl from heat and set aside. In a large bowl, lightly beat together sugar, eggs, vanilla, and salt until combined. Stir in reserved chocolate mixture. Add flour and cocoa and stir until just combined.

1. Malted Milk Brownie Bites

MAKES 60 BROWNIE BITES
WORKING TIME 20 MIN.
TOTAL TIME 1 HR.

Basic Brownie Batter

½ cup malted milk powder

1 to 2 tablespoons unsweetened cocoa powder

1. Preheat oven to 325°F. Line two 8-inch square baking pans with parchment and set aside. Combine batter and malted milk powder. Divide batter between prepared pans.

2. Bake until a skewer inserted into the center comes out with a few moist crumbs, 25 to 30 minutes. Let cool. Using a sharp knife, cut brownies into 60 one-inch pieces. Sprinkle with unsweetened cocoa powder.

2. Turtle Brownie Bars

MAKES 20 BROWNIE BARS
WORKING TIME 20 MIN. **TOTAL TIME** 1 HR.

Basic Brownie Batter

1 cup chopped peanuts

30 candy caramels, diced

⅓ cup semisweet chocolate chips, melted

2 tablespoons chopped peanuts

1 Preheat oven to 325°F. Line two 8-inch square baking pans with parchment and set aside. Mix Batter and peanuts. Divide batter between prepared pans.

2 Bake for 20 minutes, then remove pans from oven and sprinkle diced caramels over top. Continue baking until a skewer inserted into the center comes out with a few moist crumbs, about 10 minutes more. Let cool. Drizzle with melted chocolate chips and peanuts. Chill until chocolate sets, 10 minutes. Remove brownies from pan. Using a sharp knife, slice into 5 strips, then cut strips in half.

3. Rocky Road Brownies

MAKES 12 BROWNIES **WORKING TIME** 20 MIN.
TOTAL TIME 1 HR. 20 MIN.

Basic Brownie Batter

¾ cup chopped walnuts

1 cup mini marshmallows

¼ cup chopped walnuts

½ cup dark chocolate chips, melted

1 Preheat oven to 350°F. Line an 8-inch square baking pan with parchment and set aside. Stir walnuts into Batter. Pour into prepared pan.

2 Bake until a skewer inserted into the center comes out with a few moist crumbs, 45 to 50 minutes. Top with mini marshmallows and let cool. Remove brownies from pan. Top with chopped walnuts and drizzle with melted chocolate chips. Let cool on a wire rack. Using a sharp knife, cut into 12 squares.

Who says a brownie's gotta be square? Get creative with the basic size and shape, then add nuts, caramels—and even more chocolate.

4. Fudgy Peppermint Cups

MAKES 12 CUPS **WORKING TIME** 20 MIN.
TOTAL TIME 1 HR. 15 MIN.

Basic Brownie Batter

4 ounces Peppermint Patties, chopped

¼ cup semisweet chocolate chips, melted

3 (5¾-inch-long) candy canes, crushed

1 Preheat oven to 325°F. Combine Batter and chopped Peppermint Patties. Pour into a buttered and floured 12-cup muffin pan.

2 Bake until a skewer inserted into the center comes out with a few moist crumbs, 25 to 28 minutes. Let cool for 30 minutes. Remove from pan; ice tops with melted chocolate chips and sprinkle with crushed candy canes.

5. Brownie Pecan Tart

MAKES 1 TART (12 SLICES)
WORKING TIME 20 MIN. **TOTAL TIME** 1 HR.

Basic Brownie Batter

⅔ cup chopped pecans

2 tablespoons unsalted butter, melted

½ cup packed light-brown sugar

¼ cup dark syrup

½ teaspoon vanilla extract

⅛ teaspoon salt

1 Preheat oven to 350°F. Spread Batter into a buttered and floured 11-inch tart pan with a removable bottom.

2 Bake for 20 minutes. Meanwhile, in a large bowl, combine pecans, butter, sugar, syrup, vanilla, and salt. Remove tart from oven and spread mixture over top. Continue baking until a skewer inserted into the center comes out with a few moist crumbs, about 15 minutes more. Let cool before releasing tart from pan.

Sugar Cookies

A baker's best friend, this buttery, all-purpose favorite can be rolled out and cut into shapes, formed into slice-and-bake logs, or pushed through a cookie press. Let your imagination take your holiday cooking to the next level!

BASIC SUGAR-COOKIE DOUGH

MAKES 50 COOKIES **WORKING TIME** 10 MIN. **TOTAL TIME** 10 MIN.

1 stick unsalted butter, softened

1½ cups confectioners' sugar

2 large eggs

1 teaspoon vanilla extract

¼ teaspoon salt

2½ cups all-purpose flour

In a large bowl, beat together butter and confectioners' sugar using an electric mixer set on medium-high speed. Add eggs, vanilla, and salt and beat until combined. Reduce mixer speed to low, add flour, and mix until dough is smooth. Roll dough into 3 logs, 2 inches thick. Preheat oven to 350°F. Slice logs into ¼-inch-thick cookies and bake on parchment-lined baking sheets until firm and lightly browned, 8 to 10 minutes. Transfer to a wire rack and let cool.

Basic Sugar-Cookie Dough can be refrigerated for up to 5 days or frozen for up to 3 months; thaw in refrigerator before use.

Golden Honey Granola

MAKES 15 CUPS
WORKING TIME 15 MIN. **TOTAL TIME** 55 MIN.

1 (18-ounce) container old-fashioned oats (6 cups)

8 ounces sliced almonds

1 cup dried cranberries, chopped

1 cup dried apricots, chopped

1 cup light-brown sugar

1 teaspoon ground cinnamon

½ teaspoon salt

1½ sticks unsalted butter

½ cup honey

Preheat oven to 350°F. In a large bowl, toss together oats, almonds, dried fruit, sugar, cinnamon, and salt. In a small saucepan over medium heat, melt butter. Stir in honey. Pour over oat mixture and toss to distribute. Spread granola onto a parchment-lined baking pan and bake, stirring occasionally, until oats are toasted and sugar begins to caramelize, 35 to 40 minutes. Cool completely on pan. Transfer to an airtight container—like a pretty jar—and add a cute scoop for good measure.

Find recipe cards ready for your notes on pages 79-84.

Chocolate–Peanut Butter Truffles

MAKES 48 TRUFFLES
WORKING TIME 45 MIN. **TOTAL TIME** 5 HR.

8 ounces bittersweet chocolate, chopped

1 cup heavy cream

½ cup smooth peanut butter

½ teaspoon vanilla extract

¼ teaspoon salt

⅓ cup cocoa

½ cup peanuts, finely chopped

Place chopped chocolate in a medium heat-safe bowl. Set aside. In a medium saucepan over low heat, heat 1 cup heavy cream until it just begins to boil; then immediately pour over chocolate. Let sit for 1 minute. Stir until chocolate is melted and mixture is thick and smooth. Stir in peanut butter, vanilla, and salt. Pour into a shallow baking pan and refrigerate until set, 4 to 6 hours. Spoon chocolate–peanut butter mixture, by the tablespoon, into your hand and roll into balls. Place on a parchment-lined baking pan and return to refrigerator for 20 to 30 minutes. Place cocoa and peanuts in separate shallow dishes. Roll half the truffles in cocoa and the other half in peanuts, constantly shaping each ball as you work. Keep refrigerated until serving or gifting.

Vanilla Caramels

MAKES 60 PIECES
WORKING TIME 45 MIN. **TOTAL TIME** 1½ HR.

Vegetable oil, for greasing

1 cup sugar

1 cup heavy cream

½ cup unsalted butter

1 cup light corn syrup

1½ teaspoons vanilla extract

Line an 8-inch square pan with foil and generously brush with vegetable oil. Set aside. In a medium saucepan over high heat, cook sugar, without stirring, until it begins to melt and bubble. Using a metal spoon, stir slowly until sugar has completely melted, about 1 minute. Remove from heat and add cream (sugar will seize into a solid mass). Add butter and corn syrup. Fit a candy thermometer to saucepan, return to stovetop, and cook over low heat, stirring occasionally until mixture liquefies, about 30 minutes. Increase heat to medium-high and cook until caramel mixture reaches 238°F. Remove pan from heat; stir in vanilla. Carefully pour hot caramel into prepared pan. Using a spatula coated in vegetable oil, smooth any bubbles on surface. Cool caramel until firm but still slightly warm, about 35 minutes. Lift caramel from pan and peel away foil. Place on an oiled cutting board

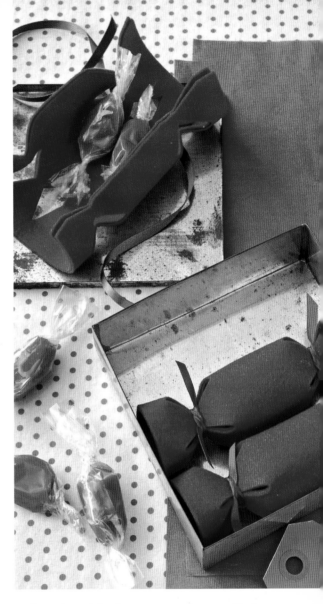

and cut into 1-inch squares, using an oiled knife. Wrap individual candies in food-safe cellophane, then tuck a few inside charming felt Christmas poppers.

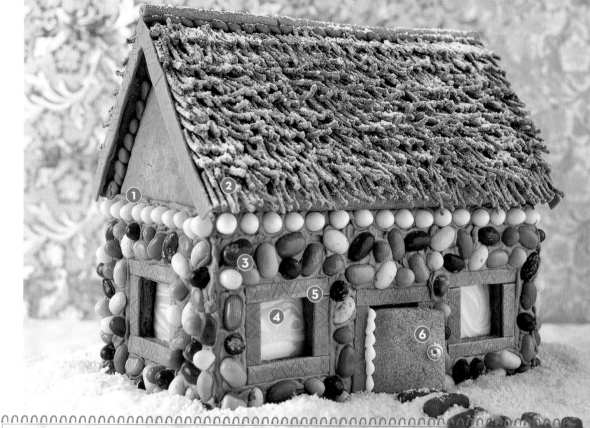

ALL THE TRIMMINGS

1 ROYAL ICING is the "glue" that holds the pieces of the house together and the exterior embellishments in place—find the recipe on page 66.

2 ROOF All-Bran cereal dusted with confectioners' sugar mimics thatching.

3 STONEWORK Assorted brown and white jelly beans, halved, create the effect of stonework.

4 WINDOWS To craft windows with a warm glow, place yellow pinwheel candies (shown on page 66) on a lightly oiled nonstick sheet pan at 350°F until just melted (about 5 to 6 minutes).

5 TRIM Sticks of red gum double the appeal of window frames and architectural details.

6 DOORKNOB A gold dragée (from amazon.com) stands in as an elegant doorknob.

Home Sweet Home

Build a charming gingerbread cottage that looks good enough to eat!

MAKES ONE 4-BY-8-INCH GINGERBREAD HOUSE **WORKING TIME** 1 HR. **TOTAL TIME** 4 HR.

6¾ cups all-purpose flour

3 tablespoons ground ginger

1½ teaspoons ground cloves

¾ teaspoon salt

1½ cups dark corn syrup

1½ cups dark brown sugar

3 sticks unsalted butter

❶ Whisk flour, ginger, cloves, and salt together in a large bowl and set aside. Combine corn syrup, brown sugar, and butter in a medium saucepan over medium heat, stirring occasionally until sugar dissolves and butter melts. Stir the syrup into flour mixture until a smooth dough forms.

❷ Cover and chill until dough is cool—about 2 hours. Roll each dough piece between 2 sheets of parchment paper to create a 12-by-10-inch rectangle about ¼-inch thick. Place rolled dough—board and all—in refrigerator and chill for 20 minutes.

❸ Use templates from pages 69-74 to cut out house pieces with a small knife—keeping dough chilled while working so cutout pieces will retain their shapes. If necessary, gather and reroll scraps until all template pieces are cut out.

❹ Carefully transfer all 6 pieces with a spatula (the house's front, back, two sides, and two halves of the roof) to 2 parchment-lined baking sheets as shown here. Chill pieces for 30 minutes before baking.

❺ Heat oven to 350°F. Bake until firm—about 35 minutes. Cool completely on a wire rack. For a smooth and even surface, place a piece of parchment on top of pieces and weight with a baking sheet while cooling.

Use the templates on pages 69-74 to cut out house pieces.

ROYAL ICING

MAKES 3 CUPS **WORKING TIME** 10 MINS. **TOTAL TIME** 10 MINS.

6 cups confectioners' sugar

4 tablespoons meringue powder

Brown food coloring

In a large bowl, beat together confectioners' sugar, meringue powder, and 3 tablespoons water using an electric mixer set on medium-high speed until very thick (tripled in volume) and smooth—about 10 minutes. Tint with food color to match gingerbread color. Cover, pressing plastic wrap directly onto icing surface, until ready to use.

Ready, Set, Build: Assembling the Cottage

❶ Find a clean, flat, sturdy piece of cardboard, foam core, or a cutting board to use as a base. (This will make it easier to transport the cottage, once completed.)

❷ Fill a piping bag fitted with a #3 tip with 1½ cups of royal icing (recipe on page 66). Holding the back wall with one hand, pipe icing along the bottom and both ends, and then join with the two sides, as shown. Press to create a tight seal. Place heavy aluminum cans (such as beans or soup) along the inside and outside of each wall to provide support. Pipe icing along the bottom and exposed edge of each side, and then attach the front of the cottage to form a rectangular box. Place additional aluminum cans inside and outside

the house if necessary to ensure that all four sides are supported. Allow the structure to dry completely (at least 3 hours).

❸ To construct the roof, pipe a thick line of royal icing along the top edge of one roof piece. Secure it to the top edge of the other roof piece so that a gable is formed. The distance between the base edges of the gable should measure about 5 inches. Stand the connected pieces on one end atop a piece of parchment or waxed paper. Pipe along the inside joint to add extra support to the connection and place heavy aluminum cans against the pieces—inside and out—to provide support while the icing dries (at least 3 hours). While the structure dries, make the windows, following the instructions on page 64.

❹ Everything must be completely dried before beginning this step. Working on one side of the house at a time, trim windows and door frames with sticks of gum. Pipe and spread icing on a small area of the facade, and cover with halved jelly bean "stones," using the photo on page 64 as a guide. Continue until each side of the exterior is covered. Then use icing to adhere the candy window panes from inside the window cutouts.

Short on time? Use our preprinted windows, front door, and other landscaping elements on pages 75-78 to decorate your house in a jiffy.

Add additional icing along the top edges of the cottage sides to attach the roof. Then pipe icing in a decorative fashion under the roof eaves. Glue cereal to the roof as "thatching" with icing, starting with a row at the bottom and continuing, row by row, to the top. Trim the roof sides and top with gum (roll the sticks into tubes for the top), using the photo on page 64 as a guide. Then give the roof a light dusting of snow—a.k.a. confectioners' sugar. Let the completed cottage dry for 12 hours before moving.

LET THE COOKING BEGIN!

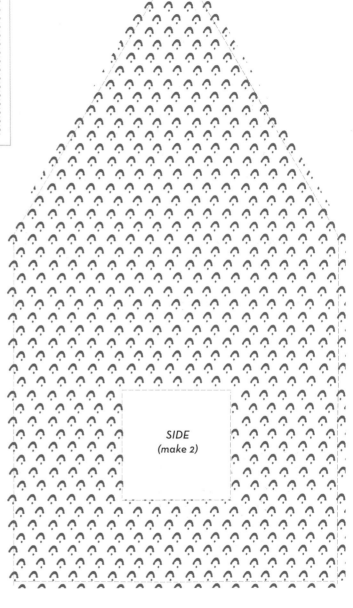

SIDE
(make 2)

GINGERBREAD COTTAGE *Punch out this template for sides, front, back, and roof pieces of the cookie house.*

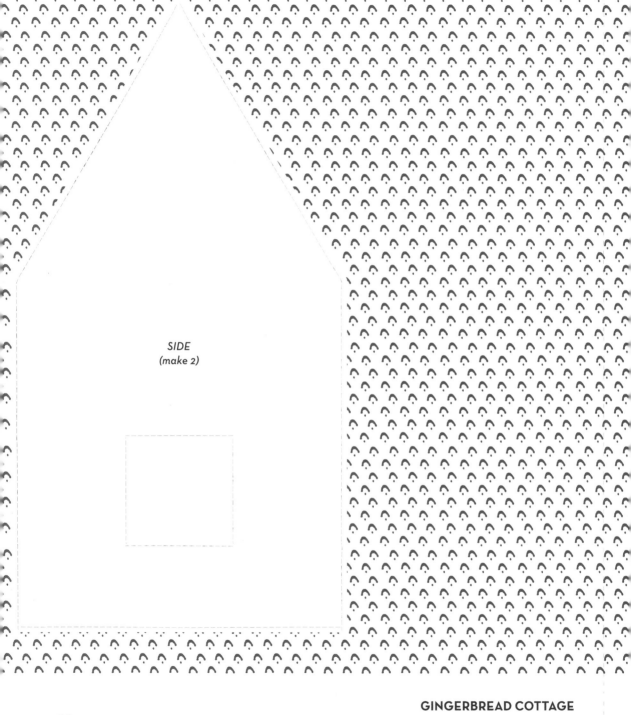

SIDE
(make 2)

GINGERBREAD COTTAGE

FRONT/BACK
(make 2)

Be sure to roll out the solid
back before creating the door
and windows for the front.
See complete instructions and
photos on pages 64-68.

GINGERBREAD COTTAGE

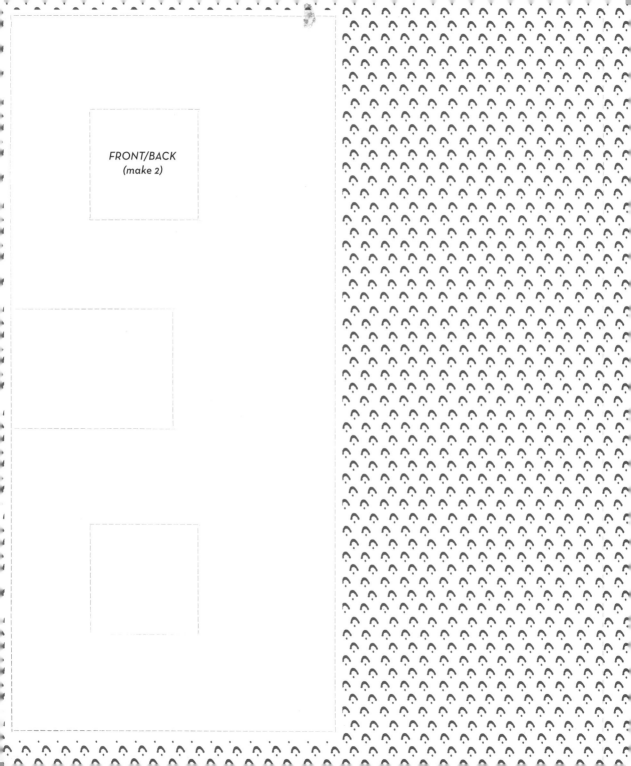

FRONT/BACK
(make 2)

ROOF
(make 2)

ROOF
(make 2)

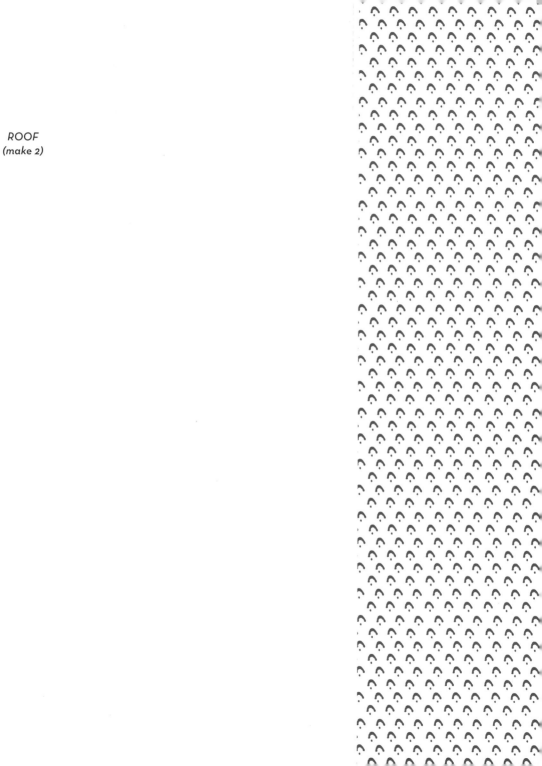

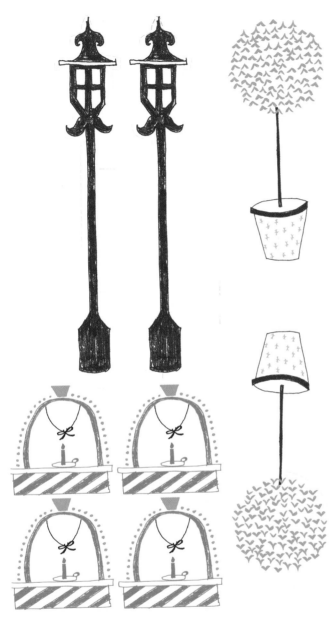

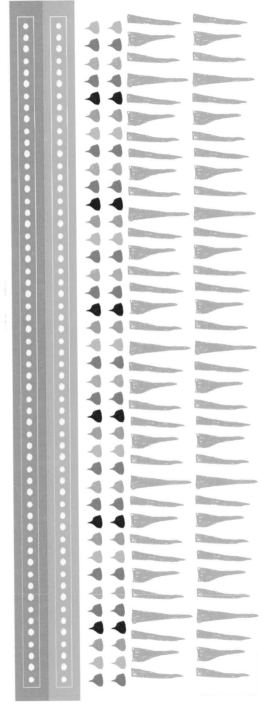

GINGERBREAD
COTTAGE DECORATIONS

To shorten the decorating time for your cottage, punch out these details.

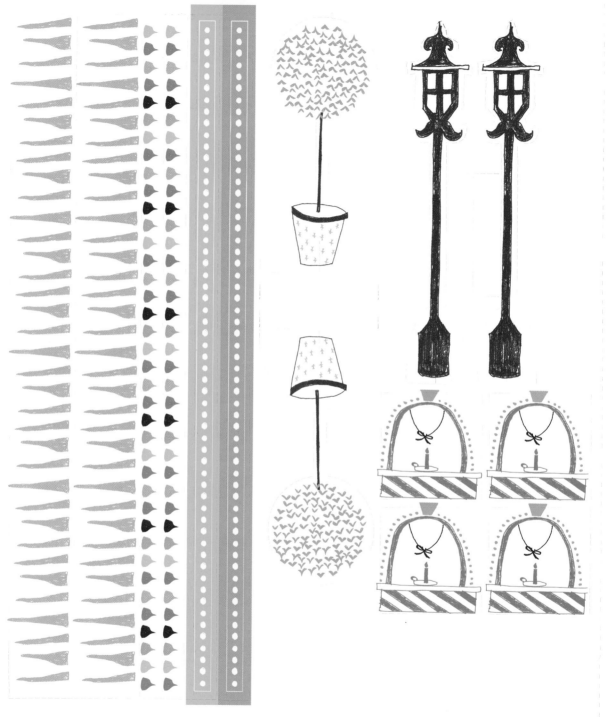

GINGERBREAD COTTAGE DECORATIONS

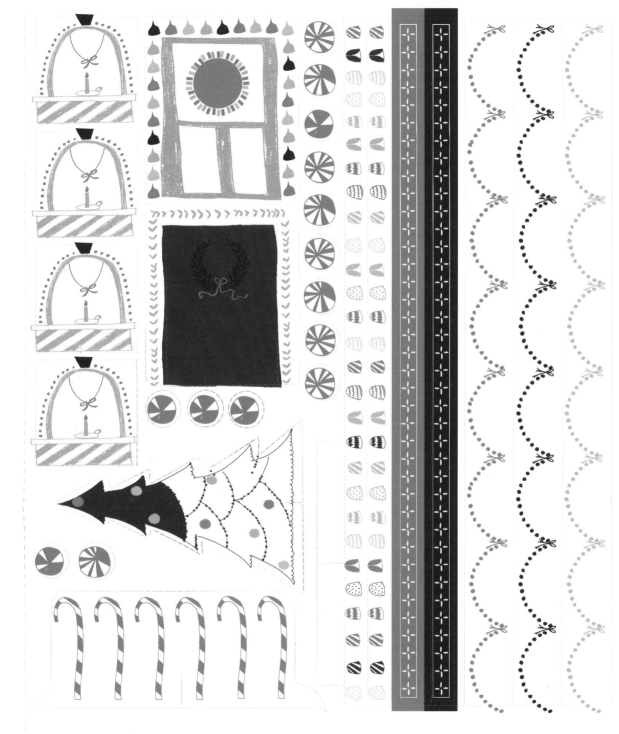

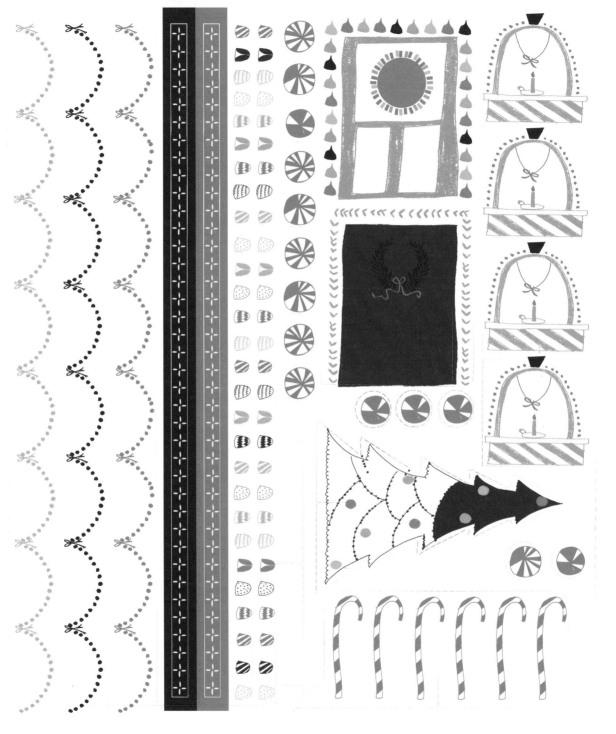

RECIPE

RECIPE

SERVES

DIRECTIONS

DIRECTIONS

RECIPE

FROM THE KITCHEN OF

RECIPE

HERE'S WHAT'S COOKIN'

SERVES

DIRECTIONS

DIRECTIONS

RECIPE

INGREDIENTS

_____
_____
_____
_____
_____
_____

_____
_____
_____
_____
_____
_____

RECIPE

_____
_____
_____
_____
_____
_____
_____
_____
_____
_____

SERVES

FROM THE KITCHEN OF

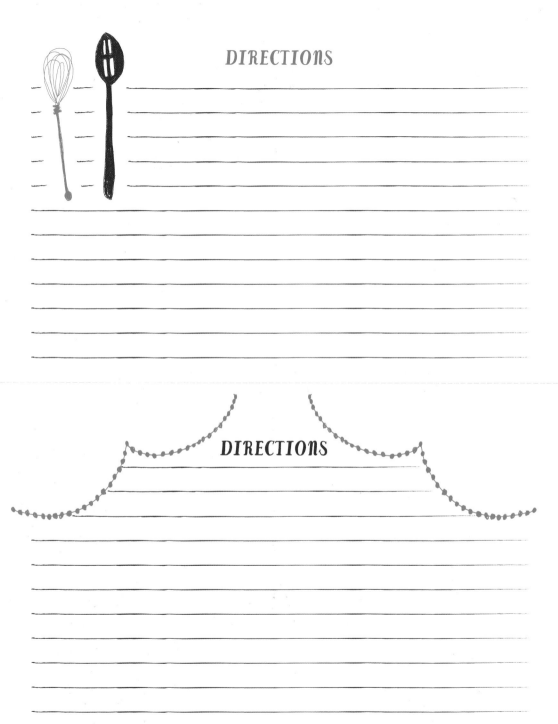

DIRECTIONS

DIRECTIONS

Made with love.   Made with love.

Made with love.   Made with love.

Made with love.   Made with love.

♥,   ♥,

♥,   ♥,

♥,   ♥,

CHAPTER

THREE

TO THE TABLE

●>>> <<<●

Dressing Up the Dining Room

EVERY FAMILY HAS A DIFFERENT WAY OF EXTENDING THE GLOW OF A momentous holiday meal. Some break out the Trivial Pursuit and other games to keep the revelry going; others linger over coffee, pie, and wine. Regardless of approach, each of these M.O.s shares a desire to celebrate one another's company, pure and simple. To reflect that sense of occasion, we've filled this chapter with ideas for turning the dining room mantle into a magical focal point, along with knock-your-socks-off centerpieces and laid-back hosting strategies. Plus, you'll find the most adorable place cards, canape flags, and napkin rings—all ready to go at a moment's notice. The only effort required by such a festive atmosphere may be gently encouraging your guests, at the end of a fabulous evening, to start winding things down.

Before

Make Over Your Mantle

Turn your fireplace into a super-festive spot with these elegant, wallet-friendly transformations.

Come December, the dining room mantle becomes a major focal point. To take ours from everyday to holiday, we decorated with items most people already have on hand this time of year, such as greeting cards, ribbons, and tissue paper. Finishing touches unearthed from the backyard (free pinecones!) give the scene a rustic feel, while inexpensive craft-store extras, like mica snow, add subtle sparkle. The result: A winter wonderland with a sophisticated look that belies its modest cost.

❶ **MIRROR** A plain mirror gains seasonal edge with this shimmering frame of tissue paper leaves. We alternated between silver and white and taped the foliage at varying angles to add dimension. To make this yourself, trace a leaf onto a piece of paper and photocopy, then cut out. Select a color scheme and spray paint your new leaves.

❷ **CANDLEHOLDERS** Small glass votives filled with pearlescent mica flakes offer an unexpected home for tapers. Provide extra stability with candle putty.

❸ **PINECONES** A few light spritzes of fake snow turn these backyard finds into frosty works of art. When they're perched underneath glass cloches misted with the same icy spray, the entire scene resembles an ultra-refined snow globe.

❹ **POINSETTIAS** What's not to love about these fuss-free flowers? Fashioned from paper, our fake blossoms—perched atop real twig stems—don't require watering and keep their cheery color all year long. Use the templates on pages 117-120.

❺ **CARDS** A pre-stretched canvas (available at art supply stores) serves as the perfect blank slate for displaying holiday greetings. Simply string ribbons across the canvas, staple in back, then hang cards from metal clips.

Want flowers fast? Pick a bunch of blooms from pages 117-120.

Nature's Bounty

Let found pinecones gathered from your backyard steal the show indoors.

For a rustic take on topiaries, place pinecones in tin cups and pedestal urns. To make the swag, start with several pinecones and a piece of braided picture-hanging wire 10 inches longer than the desired garland length. Tie each end of the wire around the two largest pinecones—cinching the wire around the center stem near the bottom, not near the ends, and twist the wire twice to secure. To fill in the garland, wrap picture-hanging wire around each pinecone toward the bottom, twist twice to secure, and leave 3-4 inches of overhang. Use the overhang to attach the pinecones to the swag, twisting tightly to secure. To hang, drape the swag over nails. Then, at the end of the season, pack the garland away for next year or use the pinecones as natural fire starters.

Clever Alternatives to the Traditional Centerpiece

Suspend your tablescape from the ceiling.

Branch out from conventional displays by using an extra-long tree limb as a platform for hanging ornaments. Simply knot lengths of twine around the branch and hang it from a row of five or six ceiling hooks.

Moving the centerpiece off the table also makes more room for cheery place cards and napkin rings—like our table-ready versions on pages 105-116.

Give larger-than-life arrangements a new home.

Free up prime dinner-table real estate by moving oversize centerpieces to the buffet. And don't bother with elaborate floral fantasies: just go "shopping" in your backyard for branches of holly, crabapple, or bittersweet berries (above). Then bring in-demand items—like butter and sauces—to the middle of the table.

Elevate the holiday spirit of dining chairs with playful angel wings.

With Santa trying to find out who's naughty or nice, why not lend your guests an angelic glow—earned or not—with a pair of feathered gliders (we found ours at ustoy.com).

Stake your "blooms" in the snow.

Fill glass vases with artificial snow—and paper flowers—for a wintry, no-wilt centerpiece.

Ta-da! Your very own cutting garden: Find flowers on pages 117-120.

A Bubbly Welcome

Keep traffic flowing in the foyer.

A no-muss, no-fuss, and no-mixers way to help revelers feel festive the moment they walk in the door: Set up a help-yourself champagne station that guests can swing by while you hang coats.

A Guide to Stocking the Ultimate Bar

Set up so you're always ready for a party!

It's inevitable this time of year—folks will be dropping by, delivering gifts, and expecting at least a little hospitality in return. Instead of panicking, prepare so that you'll be ready to fete a few unexpected visitors or throw a full-fledged bash at the drop of a hat.

① TWICE AS NICE A versatile coupe can handle both martinis and champagne; a simple old-fashioned glass serves everything else.

② ESSENTIAL ACCESSORIES For mixing, try a Boston Shaker, which comes with a pint glass that can also be called upon for stirring drinks like Manhattans or martinis, and a strainer with a fixed spring that provides a better fit to the glass. And while an ice bucket

is a no-brainer, you can make it more user-friendly by providing a generous scoop instead of tongs.

③ MIXERS AND GARNISHES Tonic water, club soda, and cola are all must-haves. From there, add juices—cranberry (for Cape Cods), orange (for screwdrivers), lemon (for Tom Collins), and lime (for margaritas). A couple of extras worth having include

aromatic bitters, a key ingredient in classic cocktails such as old-fashioneds, and dry vermouth, a martini necessity. Go-to garnishes include limes, lemons, olives, cherries, and mint.

4 THINK SMALL Mini bottles and cans look adorable—and get used up before they lose their fizz.

SPIRITS OF THE SEASON

An ideal setup involves six basic liquors, though not all need be top-shelf—especially if they're going into cocktails. Put your money toward the stuff folks drink straight-up. These suggestions come from San Francisco mixologist Greg Lindgren.

SCOTCH
Spring for a good-sipping single malt, since few people make Scotch cocktails. Our pick: Bruichladdich 12-year Second Edition.

BOURBON
Strict rules govern what can be called bourbon, so most of it's good quality, including the affordable Four Roses.

VODKA
You'll want lots of a not-too-fancy grade (like Polish brand Sobieski) because this is the most-used alcohol and one of the least likely to be consumed straight.

TEQUILA
Margaritas benefit from pricier tequila, so shell out for one made from 100 percent blue agave, like Tequila Ocho Anejo.

GIN
Though cheap gin can be awful, top-shelf isn't exquisite. So go for a midrange option like Plymouth.

RUM
For Cuba libres, try a dry white rum like Flor de Caña, since cola's already so sweet.

⑤ STORAGE-FRIENDLY SNACKS
Greet guests with an assortment of light nibbles that keep well: pistachios, a wasabi mix, crackers to serve with goat cheese, and San Francisco sommelier Shelley Lindgren's addictive nut blend (see recipe on page 103).

⑥ ONE SIZE FITS ALL
A 15-ounce wine glass does double-duty for reds and whites; a coupe is perfect for Prosecco.

⑦ PUT IT ON ICE
The recipe for well-chilled whites: an urn or bowl with a bath of two-thirds ice to one-third water. In a hurry? A teaspoon of salt speeds up the process.

THE WINE LIST

These crowd-pleasing picks don't cost a fortune—but if you really want to save, buy in bulk, since wine shops often discount cases. Plus, you'll always have an extra bottle on hand.

WHITE
Steer clear of anything noticably sweet or oaky. Didier Champalou Vouvray Sec appeals to drinkers who like a full-bodied Chablis, as well as those who enjoy a crisp Pinot Grigio.

RED
Earthly with hints of tobacco and cherry, Emilio Moro Finca Resalso tastes like a cross between Cabernet and Syrah.

SPARKLING
You'll want a Prosecco as an affordable alternative to champagne, and Bisol Prosecco di Valdobbiadene Crede Brut shines with hints of apple and pear.

Not Your Ordinary Bar Snacks

Whip up a more satisfying nut mix using fresh rosemary and a dash of paprika.

HOMEMADE SPICED NUTS (in less than 15 minutes!)

WORKING TIME 10 MIN. | **TOTAL TIME** 15 MIN.

½ pound almonds

¼ pound each hazelnuts

¼ pound each walnuts

¼ pound each pecans

¼ pound each cashews

2 tablespoons coarsely chopped rosemary

2 teaspoons salt

½ teaspoon freshly ground pepper

1 tablespoon unsalted butter, melted

2 teaspoons dark brown sugar

½ teaspoon ground paprika

¼ teaspoon ground allspice

Preheat oven to 350°F. In a large bowl, combine almonds with hazelnuts, walnuts, pecans, and cashews. Add rosemary, salt, and ground pepper and toss. Evenly spread mixture on a baking sheet. Toast in oven until nuts are light golden brown, about 10 minutes.

Meanwhile, in same mixing bowl, combine unsalted butter, melted, with dark-brown sugar, ground paprika, and ground allspice. Toss toasted nuts in brown sugar mixture.

Lucky enough to have extra pieces of pie? Corral leftovers in style with our fridge and freezer labels on page 123.

End Things On A Satisfying Note

Serve all your tasty desserts at once by setting up a separate table that guests can help themselves to in their own sweet time.

SET THE HOLIDAY TABLE

SIT HERE!

BILLY

PLACE CARDS *Punch these out to use at your next holiday fete. Just fold in half and personalize with each guest's name, nickname, or alter ego.*

HAPPY HOLIDAYS

MERRY CHRISTMAS

MERRY CHRISTMAS

WELCOME

HAPPY HOLIDAYS

MERRY CHRISTMAS

SIT HERE!

WELCOME

HAPPY HOLIDAYS

MERRY CHRISTMAS

SIT HERE!

WELCOME

HAPPY HOLIDAYS

SNOWFLAKE NAPKIN RINGS *Punch out these reversible designs to use at your next holiday fete. Just wrap each one around a rolled napkin and use tape to secure in back.*

113

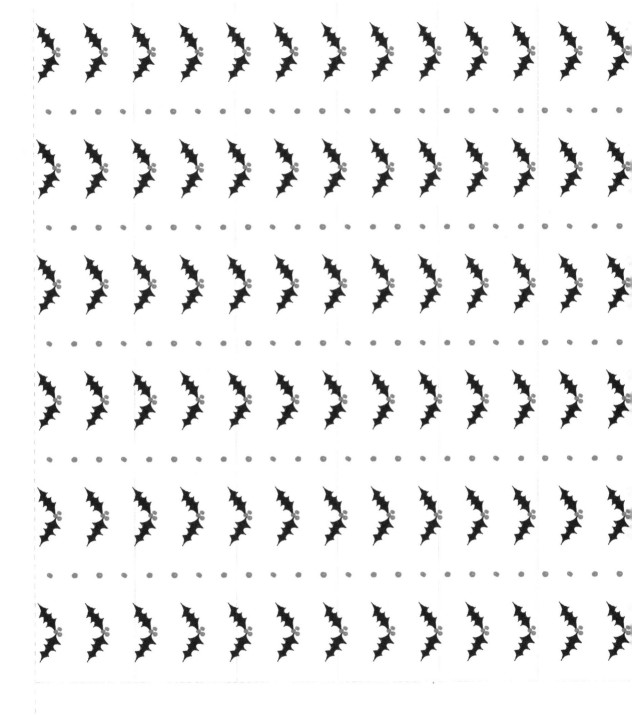

HOLLY NAPKIN RINGS

PAPER POINSETTIAS *Punch out these origami poinsettias to use as a no-wilt centerpiece, like the one shown on page 98. Push a twig through the center for a stem, and repeat for each flower.*

PAPER POINSETTIAS

PAPER POINSETTIAS

PAPER POINSETTIAS

CANAPE FLAGS

Use these stickers to turn a humble toothpick into a festive canape flag. Place toothpick in the seam where the two circles meet and match up the outside edges before smoothing together.

I *am:*

And **I** *was*
packed upon:

I *am:*

And **I** *was*
packed upon:

I *am:*

And **I** *was*
packed upon:

I *am:*

And **I** *was*
packed upon:

I *am:*

And **I** *was*
packed upon:

I *am:*

And **I** *was*
packed upon:

I *am:*

And **I** *was*
packed upon:

I *am:*

And **I** *was*
packed upon:

I *am:*

And **I** *was*
packed upon:

I *am:*

And **I** *was*
packed upon:

I *am:*

And **I** *was*
packed upon:

I *am:*

And **I** *was*
packed upon:

CHAPTER

FOUR

DAZZLING DECORATIONS

●>>> <<<●

The Thrill of Decking the Halls

IF YOU WANT TO SEE AN ADULT LIGHT UP LIKE A KID ON CHRISTMAS morning, watch their faces when it's time to unpack ornaments and other holiday accessories—the grown-up version of toys and dolls. From wreaths to stockings to tree trimmers and skirts, we'll help you blanket your home with joyful touches that will last from year to year. We've also included tons of instant ornaments to add to your collection and striking stickers to jazz up existing globes. Soon you may find yourself staying up a little later, just to stare at your tinseled evergreen. We get it. The spirit of the season starts at home.

The shining stars of this avian-themed fir? Our bird ornaments from pages 141-144.

The Ultimate Christmas Tree Doesn't Require Spending a Fortune

Let the tree-trimming begin! Find dozens of instant ornaments—including beautiful birds—on pages 141-148.

Turn vintage Audubon-style illustrations into tree-trimmers by color-copying them onto card stock, cutting out the birds, and punching holes at the tops.

Scraps of wrapping paper look pretty as a picture when tucked inside tiny frames.

Vintage baking molds add a sweet touch to any tree; simply hot-glue ribbon loops to their backs and hang.

Spray-painted white, pinecones really pop against evergreen boughs.

The looped stems of tomato pincushions make for easy hanging.

Coated in glossy white spray paint, skeleton keys feel fresh.

More Utterly Inspired Ornament Ideas

Upgrade clear glass globes.

At around a dollar each, these spheres offer an affordable catalyst for creativity. Fill one with small wooden chips, another with a single stunning peacock feather (attached to the underside of the ornament's top with hot glue). Or compose a more obvious Christmas scene by dropping a model fir tree into a globe dusted on the outside with artificial snow. You can also use tweezers to position a branch inside, then hot-glue a tiny cardinal in place.

Give delicate heirlooms pride of place.

Reserve a special spot for treasured ornaments by showcasing them inside a shadow box: Line the frame backing with bright wrapping paper, then affix your decorations with double-sided adhesive pads. <

Honor an extended—or growing— family (including pets!) with simple name tags.

These affordable cardstock hangers from an office supply store can be inscribed with favorite sayings, or as reminders of the good things that have happened over the year. And adding photographs of friends and family to your tree captures the season perfectly. >

Make these simple name tags using the punchouts on pages 153-156.

Add a Table-Top Tree (or Two)

Give side tables and windowsills a lift with a tree in every room.

Create a rustic pine-cone tree using a cone-shaped foam base from the craft store. Anchor the wide base in a container using floral clay, then wire the cones onto 2-inch-long wooden floral picks. Insert picks at a downward angle into the foam, starting at the bottom with the largest cones and working to the top with the smaller ones.

Start your own aviary using white card stock and our dove template on page 145.

5 Fresh Takes On Festive Wreaths

2. Strike harvest gold.
Slip sprigs of dried wheat into a box-wood round for a design with a subtle, Scandinavian flourish. ^

1. Reinvent the family tree.
Make your own photo grouping by using a glue gun and affixing a selection of black-and-white snapshots (use copies if you're worried about ruining the originals) to a wire wreath form. ^

3. Wind some yarn.
To craft this door adornment, first wrap Styrofoam balls (in two different sizes) and a Styrofoam wreath form with yarn. Then use a glue gun to affix balls of yarn onto the form, as shown. Note: If you're hanging your final creation outdoors, be sure to spray it with a protective finish. ^

5. Take a bough.

Give guests a fresh and abundant welcome by tucking greenery and berries inside a trapper's basket, hung on your front door. ∨

4. Think outside the circle.

Not all front-door decor requires a wreath form. To make this elegant cluster, we selected eight 4-to-6-inch pinecones and eight 2-foot-long pieces of silk ribbon. Use a glue gun to adhere the ends of each ribbon to the base of a cone. After the glue dries, collect all the ribbon ends and stagger them so that the cones fall at varying lengths. Tie the ribbon ends together in a knot, trim the tips so they are uniform, and slip the knot over a finishing nail. ∧

Add Holiday Cheer with Seasonal Pick-me-ups

Give cabinets a festive feel— jolly fast.

You can dress up kitchen cupboards with patterned wrapping paper (don't worry —it's a cinch to remove). Just cut the paper to fit behind glass cabinet doors as well as the back wall space between shelves, and use double-sided tape to affix. <

This advent calendar really stacks up.

Use ordinary grocery-store matchboxes to count down the days till Christmas. Simply glue the tops of empty boxes to one another to form rows (start with nine boxes for the base, and decrease by two until you have a single box). Cut wrapping paper to cover each section; secure with glue. Next, hot-glue the rows in a pyramid shape as shown. Use number stamps (available at craft stores) to mark the boxes 1 through 25, then fill with candy and trinkets. >

Lay your cards on the door.

This "tree" saves your mantel from a paper blizzard. To craft it, you'll need two wood dowels. Cut them into five segments, starting with 8 inches wide and enlarging each piece by 2 inches. Fold 2 yards of ribbon in half, then place the shortest dowel about 6 inches from the fold, spacing the rest about 5 inches apart from one another. Hot-glue so the dowels are sandwiched between the two ribbon tails. Attach your favorite greetings to the dowels with small binder clips, and hang.

Novel Ways to Spell Merriment

Seize the potential of unexpected supplies to broadcast your Christmas cheer.

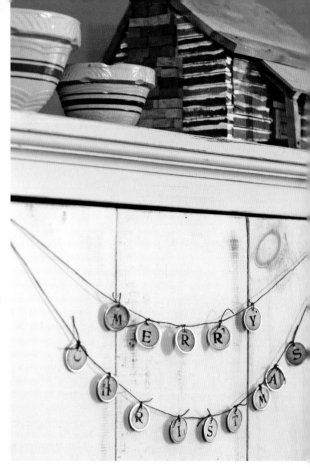

Hang it up.

Stamp out your holiday greetings using an ink pad, rubber alphabet letters, and tags from an office supply store. >

Send a Yuletide message with Scrabble tiles.

Score big with this little idea—the game's wooden letters offer a spirited way to say what's on your mind. Paint the standard holders white to really make your words pop. <

Make some merry messages with the alphabet stickers on pages 157-159.

Engage in a little pillow talk.

This trio of cushions adorned with felt letters pretty much says it all—and they're as simple to whip up as A, B, C. To upgrade store-bought throw pillows, create your own simple appliques. First, type JOY into a word-processing document, using a font you like. Enlarge each character to full letter-page size. Print, then cut out the letters and trace them onto white felt; cut out. Next, pin strips of fusible bonding web, such as Stitch Witchery, to the back of each felt letter. Center each letter (with webbing underneath) on a pillowcase and carefully remove the pins. Iron on according to the package instructions. Once the letters have adhered, add decorative stitching with embroidery thread, if desired.

Brighten a Room with Colorful Bulbs

Even unplugged lights shine when gathered in a glass apothecary jar. For a container that truly glistens, top it off with a dusting of artificial snow.

LET'S TRIM THAT TREE!

ORNAMENTAL BIRDS *Punch out these vintage Audubon-style beauties to make tree-trimmers similar to the ones shown on page 129. Punch holes at the tops for hanging.*

ORNAMENTAL BIRDS

ORNAMENTAL BIRDS

143

144

ORNAMENTAL BIRDS

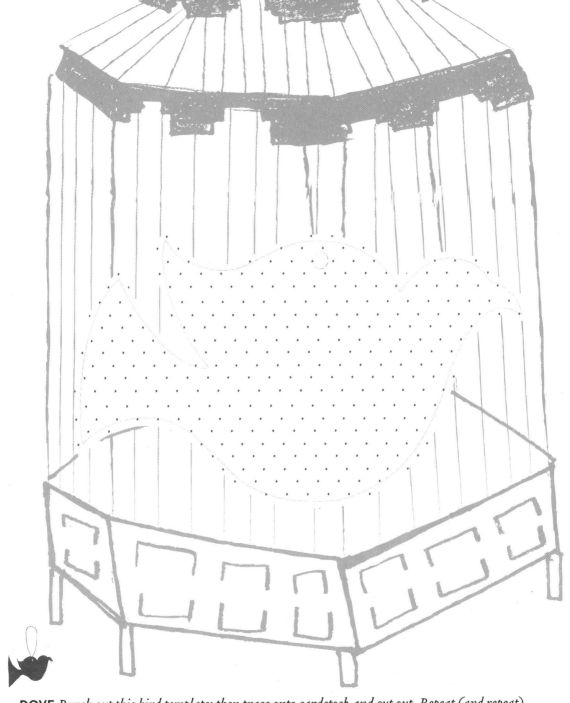

DOVE *Punch out this bird template; then trace onto cardstock and cut out. Repeat (and repeat), depending on the size of your desired flock.*

DOVE

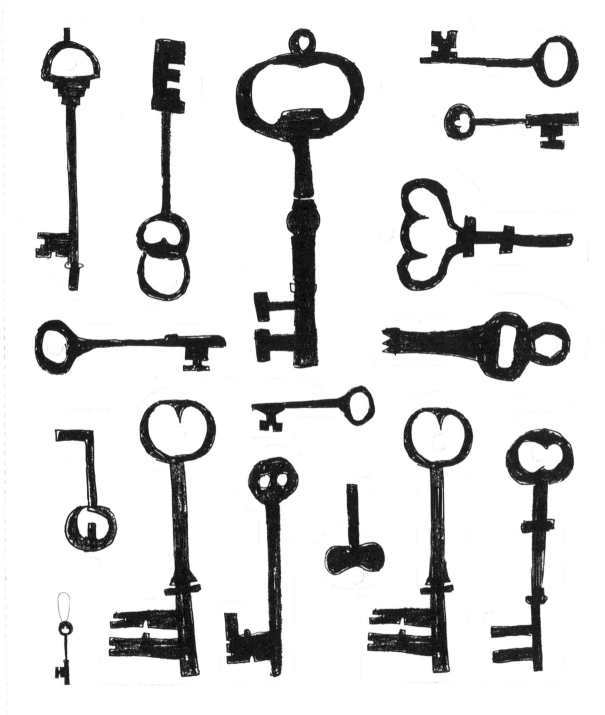

SKELETON KEYS *To unlock these ornament's full potential, punch them out and hang with ribbon.*

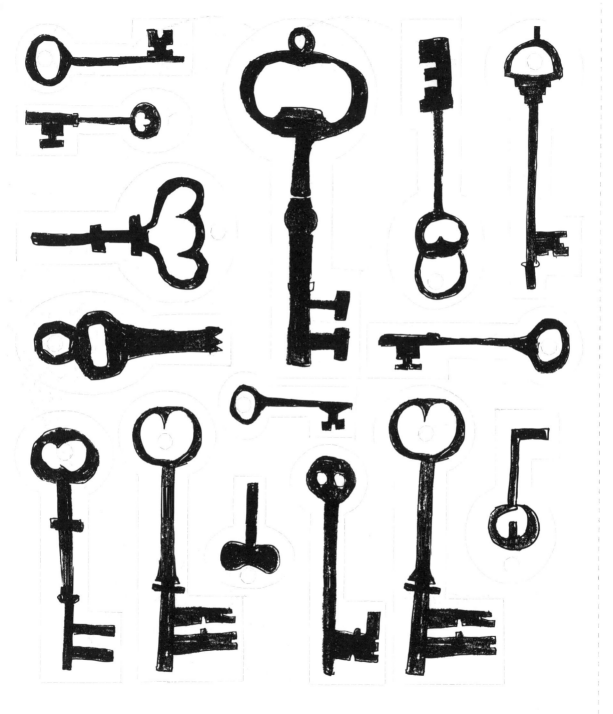

SKELETON KEYS

DISGUISES *Punch out the accessories and tape or glue each onto a chopstick to use as a Santa disguise.*

DISGUISES

DISGUISES

DISGUISES

Name:

Claim to Fame:

Name:

Claim to Fame:

FAMILY NAME TAGS
*Honor loved ones
by hanging these cards
on your tree.*

Name:

Claim to Fame:

Paste
picture
here

Paste
picture
here

Paste
picture
here

FAMILY NAME TAGS

Name:

Claim to Fame:

Name:

Claim to Fame:

Name:

Claim to Fame:

FAMILY NAME TAGS

Paste
picture
here

Paste
picture
here

Paste
picture
here

FAMILY NAME TAGS

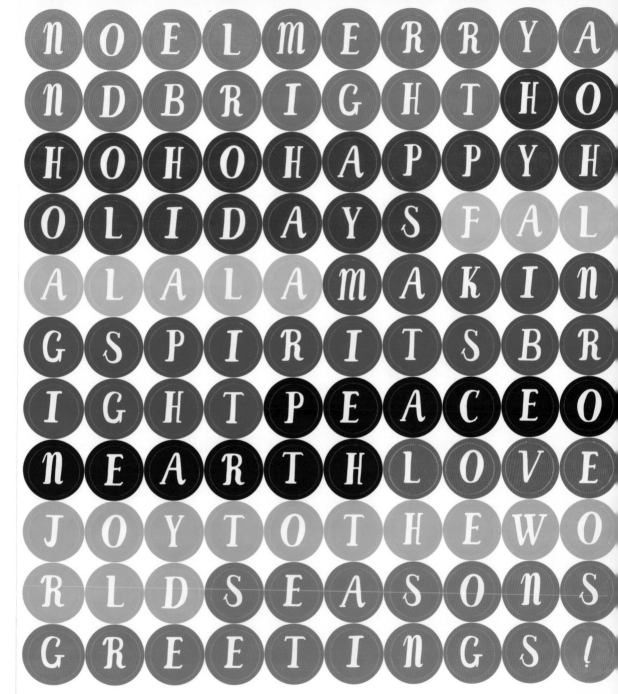

ORNAMENT STICKERS *Use the stickers on these two pages to decorate Christmas baubles and orbs. Use one of our messages or create your own!*

CHAPTER

FIVE

WRAP IT UP!

●>>> <<<●

Creative Gift Paper, Ribbons, and More

THE SHIVERS OF DELIGHT START THE MOMENT A PACKAGE APPEARS—or well before, for those determined to peer under beds and in closets in search of hidden gifts. Though the labels may identify the senders and lucky recipients clearly, mystery shrouds the identity of the items themselves. Which is why both kids and adults tiptoe up to give boxes a shake, mentally weighing and measuring the contents. Make no mistake: Pretty paper and shiny ribbons only add to this excitement, and we're going to help you drive all your loved ones mad with curiosity. (It's all in good fun.) Our gift-wrap guide will show you techniques both classic and cutting-edge—so grab your scissors and let the art of presentation begin.

First Things First: How to Wrap a Present

Where to cut? When to crease? Macy's gift-wrapping expert Belle Wesel demonstrates the definitive way—use double-sided tape!—to dress up a standard shirt box like a pro.

1 Lay the box facedown atop gift wrap, leaving paper attached to roll. Cut paper along one side, yielding a wide enough sheet to cover both sides of the box.

2 While standing on the same side of the table as the roll, pull paper tautly up and over the far end of the box. Adhere with double-sided tape, and crease paper along the box's edge with thumb and forefinger.

3 Unroll paper and bring it to meet the already wrapped end. Cut paper from roll, leaving an inch of overhang. Fold that inch under and crease along the fold. Adhere using double-sided tape.

4 Now it's time to tackle one of the open ends: Push sides of paper inward, creating four 45-degree-angle flaps, then crease along flaps.

5 Fold down top flap. Crease sharply along the top of box, then crease again where paper meets the bottom edge of box. Cut paper along that bottom crease. Adhere to the box.

6 Fold under any excess paper on the bottom flap so that it lines up perfectly with the top of box. Apply double-sided tape to the bottom flap, then fold it over top flap and adhere.

Repeat steps 4 through 6 on the box's remaining open end. Finish all sides by running your pinched thumb and forefinger along edges to create sharp lines.

Lay the wrapped box face-down on a length of ribbon (about five times as long as the box). Pull ends of ribbon up and bring right end over the left. Pull widthwise so they cross.

Turn the box over. You should have two ribbon ends of about the same length. Thread each end under the ribbon already in place, as shown.

Double-knot the ribbon, then tie into a simple bow. Use your fingers to shape the loops.

Pinch the ribbon ends lengthwise and cut at 45-degree angle to create forked ends, as shown. That's it—all wrapped up!

For presentations that really pop, punch out our gift boxes on pages 181-188.

Prettier Ways to Pack and Ship

Peppermint Pillow

Cushion items with colorful candies—a sweet gift in themselves.

Safe and Sound

Pad boxes with crumpled
sheet music (easily found at
flea markets) to ensure the
package opens on a high
note

*Make a thoughtful gift even more
adorable with one of our patterned
trinket boxes on pages 181-188.*

All-Natural

For fresh-from-
the-country
fragrance, create
a bed of greenery
and pinecones.

Wrap Stars

Six pros offer imaginative, inexpensive updates on the usual paper and bow.

Game Time

To make these winning packages, Nancy Laboz, owner of ephemera shop Parcel in Montclair, New Jersey, simply glued vintage game boards and pieces to plain boxes. "The old-school graphics look so cheerful," she says. And they're super affordable: Incomplete games often sell for only a few dollars at flea markets and garage sales.

Fine Print

You may have seen newspaper repurposed as wrapping before, but Chicago stationer Jessica Murnane's blossoming topper—which sprouts striped ribbons—keeps this classic current.

1 Stack eight sheets of newsprint and cut into an eight-inch square.

2 Accordion-fold the stack into one-inch increments.

3 Next, cut four pieces of ribbon to a length of eight inches.

4 Unfold the paper slightly and rest a piece of ribbon in each crease (if you end up with more than four folds, you'll need to cut additional ribbon).

5 Gather the folds back together and pinch the center of the paper tightly (it will look like a bow tie), binding it with a rubber band.

6 Starting from the top, peel up each layer of newspaper, scrunching it together as you go. Finally, curl the ribbon to make a cluster in the topper's center.

A Splash of Color

Got a box of crayons? Then you can replicate New York City graphic designer Adrienne Wong's abstract print. The artist channeled her inner grade-schooler by sandwiching colorful wax shavings between layers of tissue paper (two on the top and two on the bottom) and ironing them until the wax melted. After wrapping, Wong adorned the gift with an asymmetrically placed satin ribbon and a cluster of tissue dahlias (instructions on opposite page).

CRAFT ADRIENNE WONG'S DELICATE DAHLIAS

SUPPLIES

Tissue paper

Crayons

Newspaper

Iron

String

1 Sandwich crayon shavings between tissue paper—two sheets on top and two on the bottom. Protect with a piece of newspaper and iron on medium heat.

2 Remove newspaper; then separate all four sheets of tissue. Cut one piece to 4" x 6"; a second to 5" x 6"; and a third to 6" x 6" (discard the fourth piece).

3 Accordion-fold each of the three sheets into half-inch increments. Trim so each stack has rounded ends (Fig. 1).

4 Unfold and stack the sheets atop each other as shown (Fig. 2). Cinch the middle lengthwise with string and knot; then gently pull tissue up and toward the center. Scrunch to form petals.

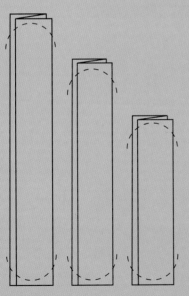

(Fig. 1)

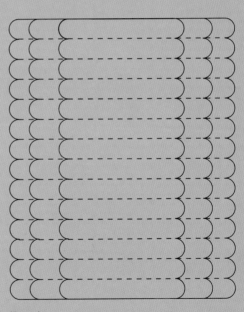

(Fig. 2)

Shadow Boxes

To follow the shining example of New York City's Minhee Cho, owner of stationery store Paper+Cup: Wrap gifts in tissue paper, paste holiday-themed silhouettes on top (Cho found these in a clip-art book), and cover each box in a glossy layer of cellophane. Adding TO and FROM speech bubbles next to the reindeer eliminates the need for a gift tag.

Shortcut! Use our silhouettes on pages 177-180 to pull this look together in a snap.

Mix Tape

Kraft paper gets a kick from brightly hued masking tape, which San Diego-based graphic designer Joy D. Cho layered in alternating horizontal and vertical strips. The crowning glory: paper straws that she frayed at the ends, then tied together with bakery twine, to resemble a snowflake.

Music to the Eyes

This *Jingle Bells* sheet music cost $15 at an antiques store, but it yielded an endless supply of wrapping paper, says Karen Bartolomei of New York City, owner of Grapevine Invitations and author of *Paperie for Inspired Living*. She enlarged the music on a copier, then printed it onto thick paper. A satin bow and jumble of—what else?—jingle bells provide the finishing touches.

Let the creativity continue with decorative coupons—you can tailor to your recipient—on pages 189-192. We've also created silhouette gift tags like those shown. Find them on pages 177-180.

Go Beyond Red and Green

These ultra-elegant boxes make use of multitasking paper you can use all year—not just during the holidays—along with tiny ornaments that bump up the Christmas factor.

Skirted Pleasure

A literal take on the Christmas tree skirt, this resourceful project makes clever use of old duds gathering dust in your closet. All you need are two kilts (or other pleated skirts) in complementary colors.

OPERATION SANTA'S WORKSHOP

SILHOUETTE TAGS *Punch out these cards to mimic the look featured on page 175.*

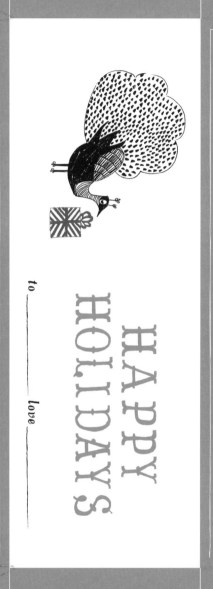

HAPPY
HOLIDAYS

to

_____

love

_____

GIFT BOXES *Cut, fold, and tape to use for gifting trinkets.*

GIFT BOXES

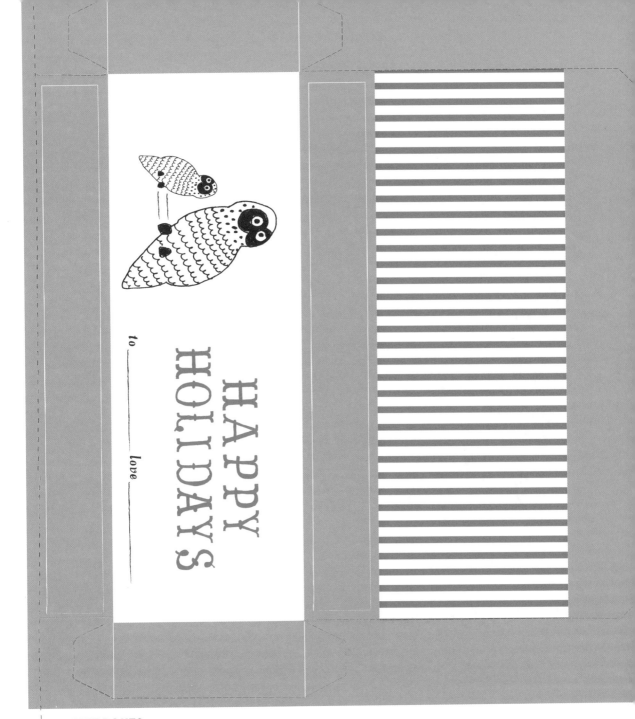

HAPPY HOLIDAYS

to _____

love _____

GIFT BOXES

HAPPY HOLIDAYS

love

to

GIFT BOXES

HAPPY HOLIDAYS

to

love

GIFT BOXES

I.O.U. COUPON

To: _____

With love: _____

The promise: _____

_____

_____

HOMEMADE COUPONS *Offer your recipient a tailored gift certificate for a shopping trip, home-made goodies—or perhaps a chore around the house. Just fill out the coupon, and punch out, then fold this self-enclosing envelope, using tape to secure.*

HOMEMADE COUPONS

I.O.U. COUPON

To: _____

With love: _____

The promise: _____

_____

_____

HOMEMADE COUPONS

HOMEMADE COUPONS

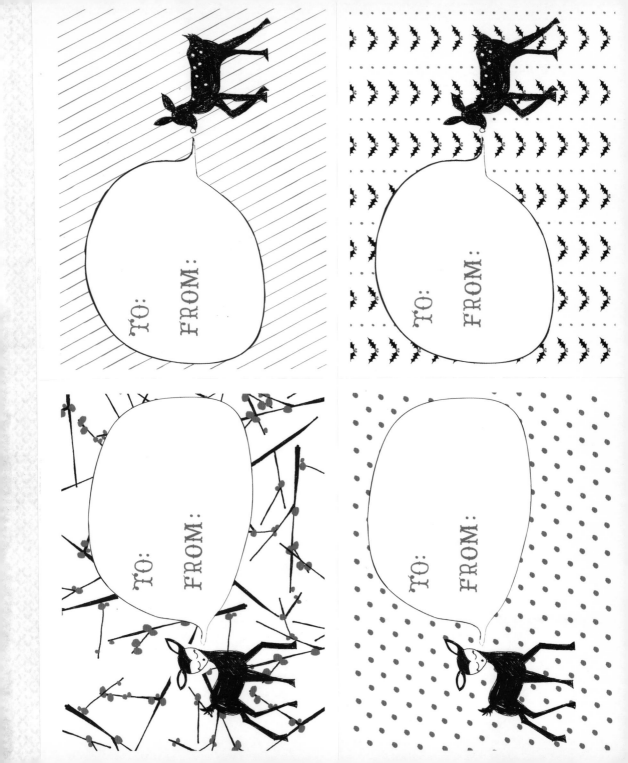

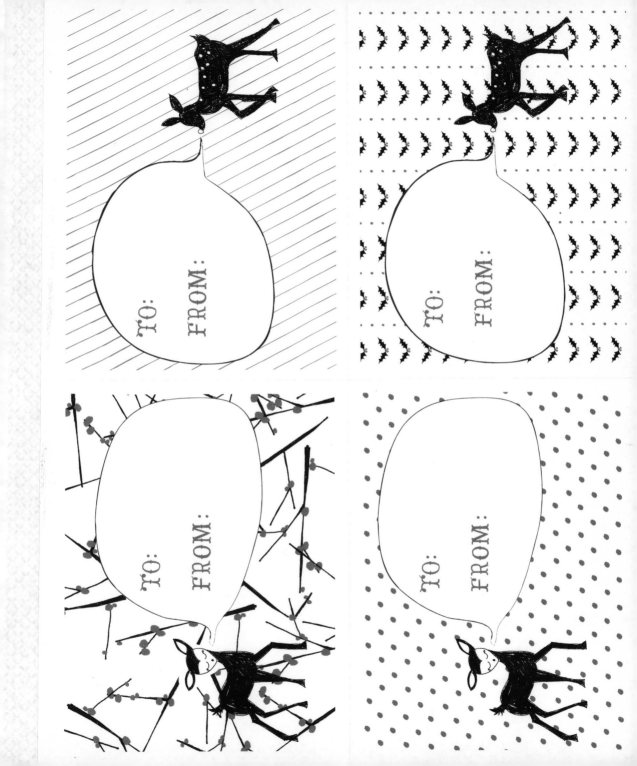